Track Finder

by
illu

A Guide to Mammal Tracks of Eastern North America

NATURE STUDY GUILD PUBLISHERS
A division of Keen Communications, Birmingham, AL

D0019919

To use this book

1. Select a typical section of track. An animal's gait will vary, but it has one preferred speed.

2. If you find:
   - a good track, go to page 4
   - a good, clear print, go to page 6

   Also read the clues on pages 2 and 3

3. Remember that tracks are only clues and it is not always possible to identify the track to species.

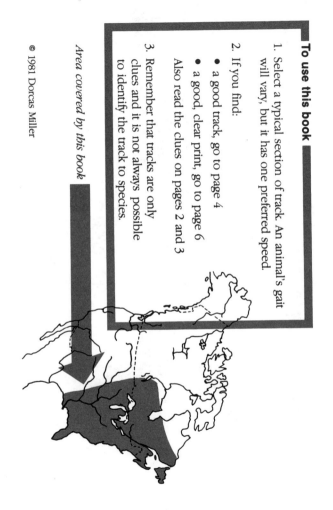

Area covered by this book

Tracking terms

Print: impression made by one foot

Track: series of prints

Straddle: width of track

Stride: distance between prints of walking animal

Leap: distance between sets of four prints made by hopping or bounding animal

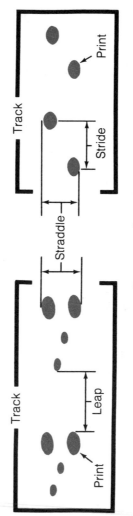

→ *Direction of travel* →

Sizes given are averages for adult animals. (Remember that even human foot sizes vary!) A footprint may look different on sand than it does in loose snow. Be observant, and use the clues and ranges given in this book to help make decisions.

A single, wide trough in snow, try:

- otter, p 31
- skunk, p 52-53
- porcupine, p 57
- beaver, p 58

Two narrow troughs in snow, try:

- deer, p 14
- moose, p 15

Gnawed branches with teeth marks:

- less than 2mm wide, try mice, p 36-37
- 2-4mm wide, try rabbits, p 42-43
- large gnawed area with clean edges and irregular outline, may be high in tree, try porcupine, p 57

Gnawed nuts, try squirrels, p 38-41

Scat composed of fur, bones, feathers, try:

- canines, p 16-19
- felines, p 20-21
- weasel family, p 26-31

Scat composed of sawdust-like vegetative matter, try:

- deer, p 14
- moose, p 15
- rabbits, p 42-43
- hares, p 44-45
- porcupine, p 57

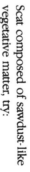

Scat or urine deposited on a rock, on a log, or in a path, try canines, p 16-19, or weasels, p 26-27.

Softwood twigs littering the ground, try:

- squirrels, p 38-41
- porcupine, p 57

Claw marks on trees, bark stripped away from trunk, old logs ripped apart, try bear, p 59

Small tracks leading from tree to tree, try squirrels, p 38-41

Tracks leading from garbage can to garbage can, try raccoon, p 53

Tracks leading into snow tunnel, try:

- voles, p 24-25
- weasels, p 26-27
- mink, p 28

Twig ends:

- severed with one sharp cut, try hares, p 44-45

- severed with several sharp cuts, try rabbits, p 42-43

- ragged, chewed by molars rather than incisors, try deer, p 14

Perfect walking

If the track looks like a nearly straight line of prints like this...

...or this,

the animal is a perfect walker. It places the hind foot almost exactly in the print made by the front foot. The track has a narrow straddle and a simple pattern. It is characteristic of canines, felines, and hoofed animals. Go to p 12

Imperfect walking

If prints overlap to form a zig-zag or if prints are paired large/small like this...

...or this,

the animal is an imperfect walker. It places the hindfoot on the palm of the front print or in a new spot altogether. The straddle is wide compared to perfect walkers. Heavyset, squat animals like raccoon, bear, and skunks are in this group. Go to p 46

This classification of four basic track patterns was developed by Donald Stokes in A GUIDE TO NATURE IN WINTER (Little, Brown and Company) and is used here with his permission.

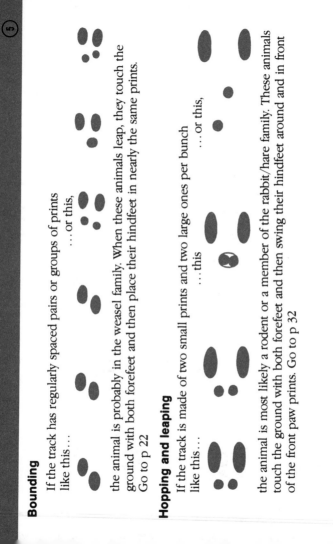

Bounding

If the track has regularly spaced pairs or groups of prints like this...   ...or this,

the animal is probably in the weasel family. When these animals leap, they touch the ground with both forefeet and then place their hindfeet in nearly the same prints. Go to p 22

Hopping and leaping

If the track is made of two small prints and two large ones per bunch like this...   ...this   ...or this,

the animal is most likely a rodent or a member of the rabbit/hare family. These animals touch the ground with both forefeet and then swing their hindfeet around and in front of the front paw prints. Go to p 32

It is difficult to identify an animal by a single print. A print's shape is influenced by the surface it's made on and by the animal's gait. Front and rear prints of the same animal may differ. This print key uses the lengths of the largest prints, whether front or rear. If this key gives you an unreasonable answer (badgers in Virginia are unreasonable) try again.

If print has:

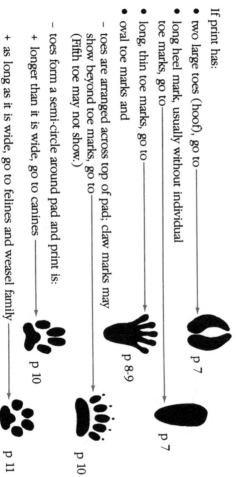

- two large toes (hoof), go to ———— p 7

- long heel mark, usually without individual toe marks, go to ———— p 7

- long, thin toe marks, go to ————

- oval toe marks and

- toes are arranged across top of pad; claw marks may show beyond toe marks, go to ———— (Fifth toe may not show.)

- toes form a semi-circle around pad and print is:

+ longer than it is wide, go to canines ————

+ as long as it is wide, go to felines and weasel family ————

p 8-9

p 7

p 10

p 10

p 11

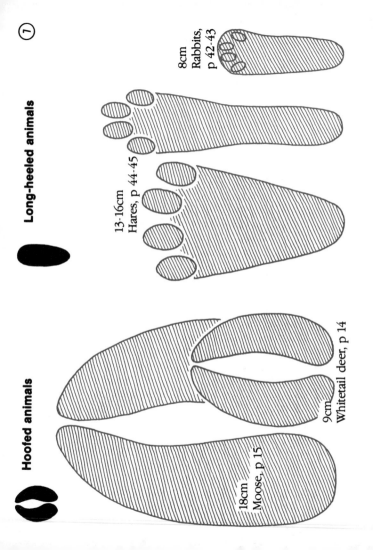

⑦

Hoofed animals

18cm
Moose, p 15

9cm
Whitetail deer, p 14

Long-heeled animals

13-16cm
Hares, p 44-45

8cm
Rabbits,
p 42-43

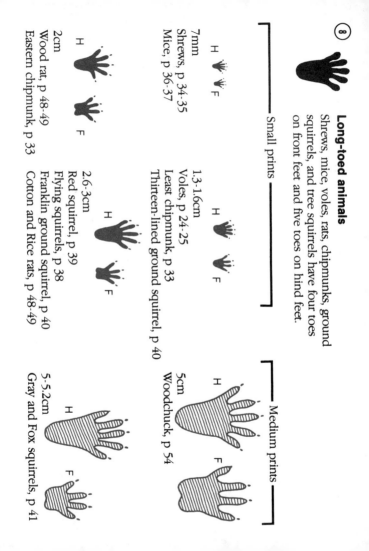

Long-toed animals

Shrews, mice, voles, rats, chipmunks, ground squirrels, and tree squirrels have four toes on front feet and five toes on hind feet.

Small prints

7mm
Shrews, p 34-35
Mice, p 36-37

H F

2cm
Wood rat, p 48-49
Eastern chipmunk, p 33

H F

1.3-1.6cm
Voles, p 24-25
Least chipmunk, p 33
Thirteen-lined ground squirrel, p 40

H F

2.6-3cm
Red squirrel, p 39
Flying squirrels, p 38
Franklin ground squirrel, p 40
Cotton and Rice rats, p 48-49

H F

Medium prints

5cm
Woodchuck, p 54

H F

5-5.2cm
Gray and Fox squirrels, p 41

H F

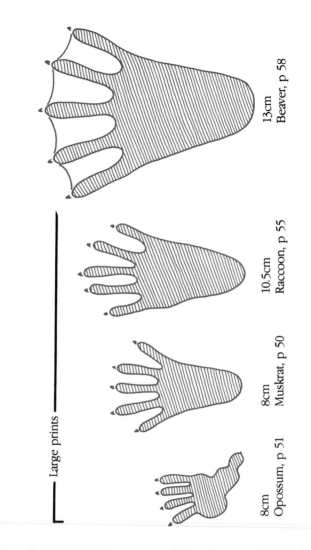

9

Large prints

13cm
Beaver, p 58

10.5cm
Raccoon, p 55

8cm
Muskrat, p 50

8cm
Opossum, p 51

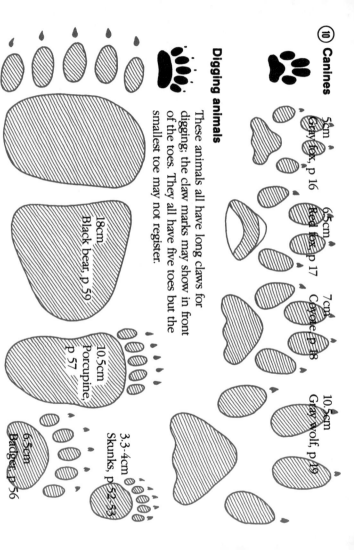

5cm
Gray fox, p 16

6.5cm
Red fox, p 17

7cm
Coyote, p 18

10.5cm
Gray wolf, p 19

Digging animals

These animals all have long claws for digging; the claw marks may show in front of the toes. They all have five toes but the smallest toe may not register.

18cm
Black bear, p 59

10.5cm
Porcupine, p 57

3.3-4cm
Skunks, p 52-53

6.5cm
Badger, p 56

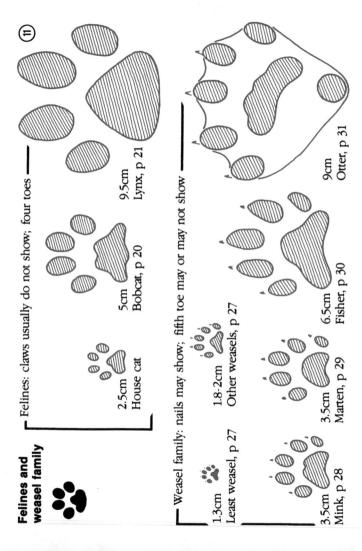

Felines and weasel family

Felines: claws usually do not show; four toes

2.5cm
House cat

5cm
Bobcat, p 20

9.5cm
Lynx, p 21

Weasel family: nails may show; fifth toe may or may not show

1.3cm
Least weasel, p 27

1.8-2cm
Other weasels, p 27

3.5cm
Marten, p 29

6.5cm
Fisher, p 30

9cm
Otter, p 31

3.5cm
Mink, p 28

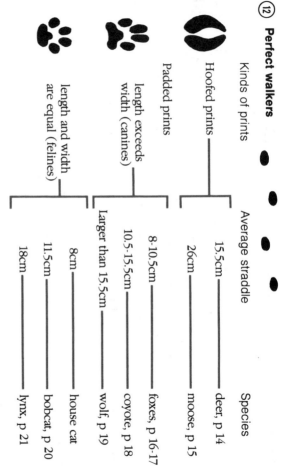

Kinds of prints		Average straddle	Species
Hoofed prints		15.5cm	deer, p 14
		26cm	moose, p 15
Padded prints	length exceeds width (canines)	8-10.5cm	foxes, p 16-17
		10.5-15.5cm	coyote, p 18
		Larger than 15.5cm	wolf, p 19
	length and width are equal (felines)	8cm	house cat
		11.5cm	bobcat, p 20
		18cm	lynx, p 21

Dogs have prints like other canines but unless they're trained hunters, they're not perfect walkers. They usually leave erratic tracks with varied gaits, often with toe drags. Canines frequently show toenails in a clear print. Felines usually keep claws retracted, so claws do not show in prints.

GAITS OF PERFECT WALKERS

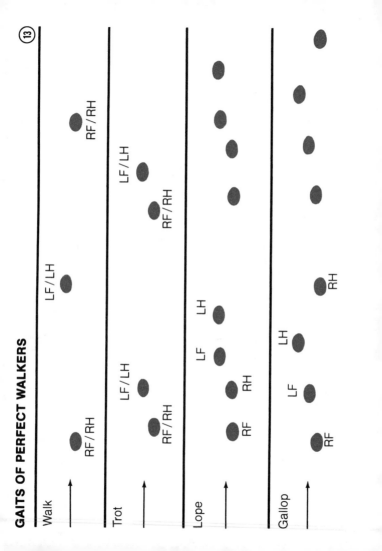

Walk

RF/RH   LF/LH   LF/LH   RF/RH

Trot

RF/RH   LF/LH   LF/LH   RF/RH

Lope

RF   RH   LF   LH

Gallop

RF   LF   LH   RH

⑬

Whitetail Deer
Odocoileus virginianus

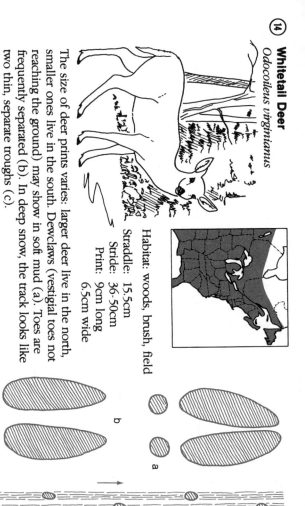

Habitat: woods, brush, field
Straddle: 15.5cm
Stride: 36-50cm
Print: 9cm long
6.5cm wide

The size of deer prints varies: larger deer live in the north, smaller ones live in the south. Dewclaws (vestigial toes not reaching the ground) may show in soft mud (a). Toes are frequently separated (b). In deep snow, the track looks like two thin, separate troughs (c).

Mule deer (*Odocoileus hemionus*) is a western deer whose tracks may be found in the open country of Minnesota and Iowa. Prints are like those of whitetail deer.

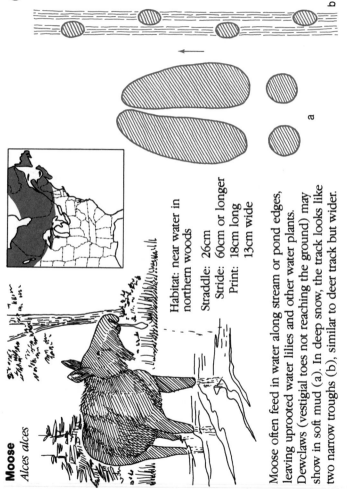

Moose
Alces alces

Habitat: near water in
northern woods

Straddle: 26cm
Stride: 60cm or longer
Print: 18cm long
13cm wide

Moose often feed in water along stream or pond edges, leaving uprooted water lilies and other water plants. Dewclaws (vestigial toes not reaching the ground) may show in soft mud (a). In deep snow, the track looks like two narrow troughs (b), similar to deer track but wider.

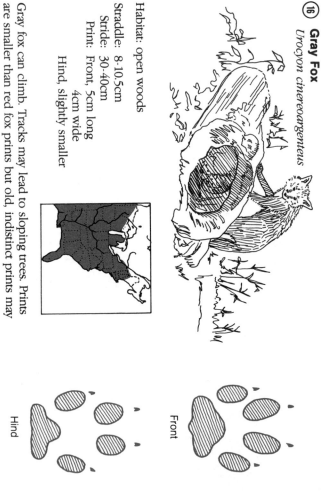

16 Gray Fox
Urocyon cinereoargenteus

Habitat: open woods
Straddle: 8-10.5cm
Stride: 30-40cm
Print: Front, 5cm long
4cm wide
Hind, slightly smaller

Gray fox can climb. Tracks may lead to sloping trees. Prints are smaller than red fox prints but old, indistinct prints may look alike.

Front

Hind

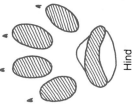

Front

Hind

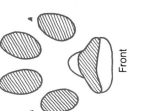

Habitat: open woods, field edge

Straddle: 8-10.5cm
Stride: 30-40cm
Print: Front, 6.5cm long
5cm wide
Hind, slightly smaller

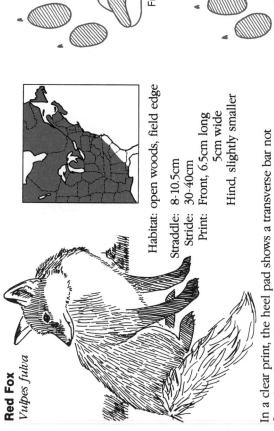

Red Fox
Vulpes fulva

In a clear print, the heel pad shows a transverse bar not found in other canines.

Arctic fox (*Alopex lagopus*) has a similar but slightly larger print, stride, and straddle; lives in northern Canada, including parts of Quebec and Labrador.

⑱ Coyote
Canis latrans

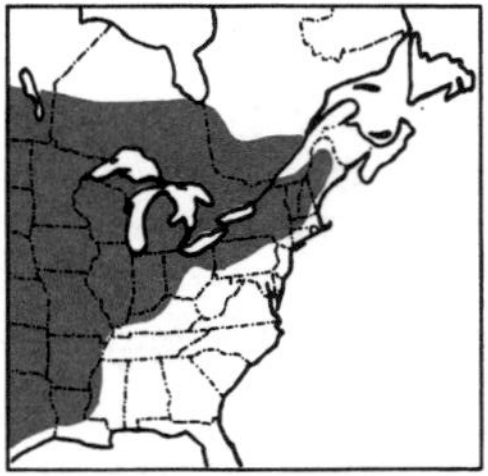

Habitat: open woods, brush
Straddle: 10.5-15.5cm
Stride: 30-40cm
Print: Front, 7cm long
6cm wide
Hind, slightly smaller

Coyote range has been steadily expanding eastward. Red wolf (*Canis niger*) is an endangered species found in bottomland, brush, and forested areas of southwest Louisiana. Tracks and prints are similar to those of coyote.

Hind

Front

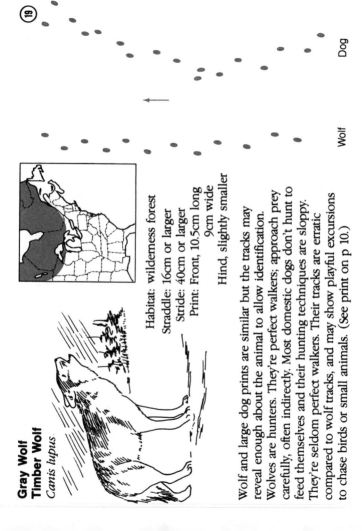

Dog

Wolf

Gray Wolf
Timber Wolf
Canis lupus

Habitat: wilderness forest
Straddle: 16cm or larger
Stride: 40cm or larger
Print: Front, 10.5cm long
9cm wide
Hind, slightly smaller

Wolf and large dog prints are similar but the tracks may reveal enough about the animal to allow identification. Wolves are hunters. They're perfect walkers; approach prey carefully, often indirectly. Most domestic dogs don't hunt to feed themselves and their hunting techniques are sloppy. They're seldom perfect walkers. Their tracks are erratic compared to wolf tracks, and may show playful excursions to chase birds or small animals. (See print on p 10.)

⑳ Bobcat
Lynx rufus

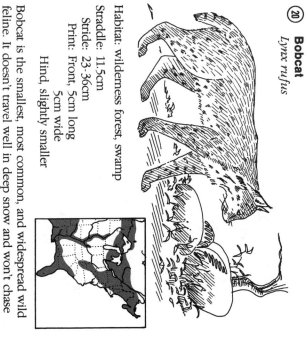

Habitat: wilderness forest, swamp
Straddle: 11.5cm
Stride: 23-36cm
Print: Front, 5cm long
     5cm wide
    Hind, slightly smaller

Bobcat is the smallest, most common, and widespread wild feline. It doesn't travel well in deep snow and won't chase prey through it. Domestic cat print is much smaller, about half the size of bobcat's, and is found near homes and towns.

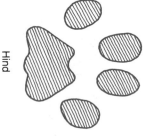

Hind

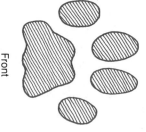

Front

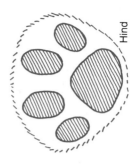

Front

Hind

Canada Lynx
Lynx canadensis

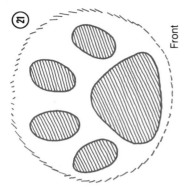

Habitat: wilderness forest, swamp

Straddle: 18cm

Stride: 26-36cm

Print: Front, 9.5cm long
9.5cm wide

Hind, slightly smaller

In winter, when lynx grows thick hair on the bottoms of its paws, its prints are circular depressions without clear toe marks.

Mountain lion or cougar (*Felix concolor*) is an endangered species which inhabits wilderness swamps of Florida, Louisiana, Arkansas, and possibly other areas in the east. Its prints—which are similar to those of lynx but smaller and without thick winter hair—are rarely seen.

22 BOUNDERS

Average straddle	Clues	Species
3cm	Very tiny double print, in winter usually leading to snow tunnel	voles and lemmings, p 24-25
4cm	Limited range; tracks leading to snow tunnel	least weasel, p 26-27
8cm	Tracks leading to snow tunnel, but not directly into water	other weasels, p 26-27
6-9cm	Tracks leading directly into snow tunnel or into water	mink, p 28
8-12cm	Tracks in deep snow are like elongated diamonds	squirrels, p 38-41
9-10.5cm	Tracks leading to tree (uncommon because marten is arboreal)	marten, p 29
15.5cm or larger	Limited range	fisher, p 30
21-26cm	Tracks leading to trough or slide	otter, p 31

Weasel family members (all above species except voles, lemmings, and squirrels) show great variation in size from individual to individual, especially because males of each species are larger than females. Note range and other clues.

GAITS OF BOUNDERS

Bounding pattern may grade into or out of other patterns.

Bounding

● LF/LH   ● LF/LH   ● LF/LH

● RF/RH   ● RF/RH   ● RF/RH

Walking

● RF/RH   ● LF/LH   ● LF/LH

● RF/RH

Loping

LH

LF   RF

RH

Running

LH

LF

RF   RH

(23)

Meadow Vole
Field Mouse
Microtus pennsylvanicus

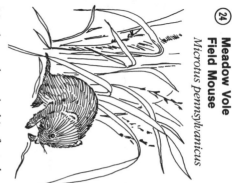

Habitat: lake, stream,
marsh edge; overgrown
grassland; orchard

Straddle: 3cm
Leap: 8-9cm
Print: 1.3cm long
1.3cm wide

Prints in mud

Meadow vole and white-footed mice (pages 36-37) leave most of the little tracks found in winter. Tracks of other voles and lemmings (page 25) are similar to those of meadow vole. Voles often travel in snow tunnels for protection.

Voles sometimes leave tail marks. Lemmings have short tails and don't leave tail marks.

Prints in snow

Running in snow

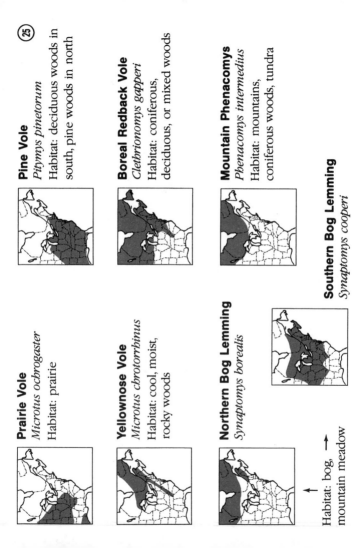

Pine Vole
Pitymys pinetorum
Habitat: deciduous woods in south, pine woods in north

Boreal Redback Vole
Clethrionomys gapperi
Habitat: coniferous, deciduous, or mixed woods

Mountain Phenacomys
Phenacomys intermedius
Habitat: mountains, coniferous woods, tundra

Prairie Vole
Microtus ochrogaster
Habitat: prairie

Yellownose Vole
Microtus chrotorrhinus
Habitat: cool, moist, rocky woods

Northern Bog Lemming
Synaptomys borealis

Habitat: bog, ← mountain meadow

Southern Bog Lemming
Synaptomys cooperi

Shorttail Weasel

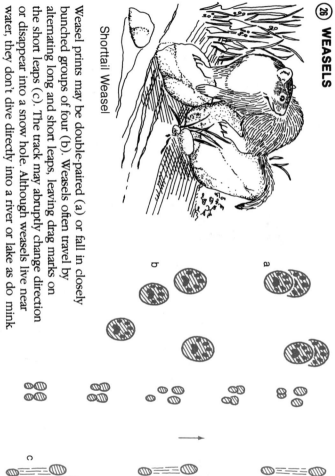

Weasel prints may be double-paired (a) or fall in closely bunched groups of four (b). Weasels often travel by alternating long and short leaps, leaving drag marks on the short leaps (c). The track may abruptly change direction or disappear into a snow hole. Although weasels live near water, they don't dive directly into a river or lake as do mink.

Longtail Weasel
Mustela frenata

Habitat: all land habitats near water

Straddle: 8cm
Leap: 50-130cm
Print: 2cm long
2cm wide

Shorttail Weasel Ermine
Mustela erminea

Habitat: woods near streams

Straddle: 8cm
Leap: 30-100 cm
Print: 1.8cm long
1.8cm wide

Least Weasel
Mustela rixosa

Habitat: open woods, field

Leap: 20-30cm usual, up to 60cm
Print: 1.2-1.4cm long
1-1.1cm wide

It's very difficult to tell longtail weasel from shorttail weasel tracks because the prints and the lengths of leap are similar. Both species can climb trees, though they spend most of their time on the ground.

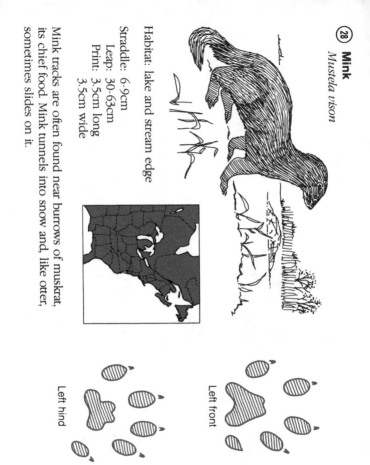

28 Mink
Mustela vison

Habitat: lake and stream edge

Straddle: 6-9cm
Leap: 30-63cm
Print: 3.5cm long
3.5cm wide

Mink tracks are often found near burrows of muskrat, its chief food. Mink tunnels into snow and, like otter, sometimes slides on it.

Left front

Left hind

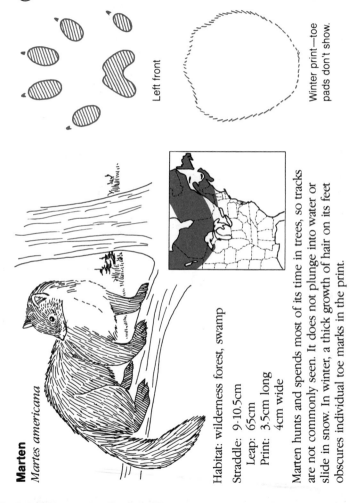

Left front

Winter print—toe pads don't show.

Marten
Martes americana

Habitat: wilderness forest, swamp

Straddle: 9-10.5cm
Leap: 65cm
Print: 3.5cm long
4cm wide

Marten hunts and spends most of its time in trees, so tracks are not commonly seen. It does not plunge into water or slide in snow. In winter, a thick growth of hair on its feet obscures individual toe marks in the print.

Fisher
Pekans
Martes pennanti

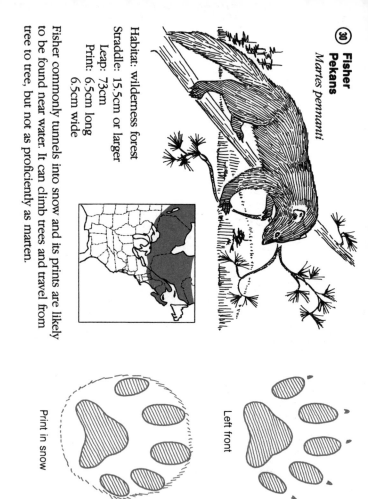

Habitat: wilderness forest
Straddle: 15.5cm or larger
Leap: 73cm
Print: 6.5cm long
6.5cm wide

Fisher commonly tunnels into snow and its prints are likely to be found near water. It can climb trees and travel from tree to tree, but not as proficiently as marten.

Left front

Print in snow

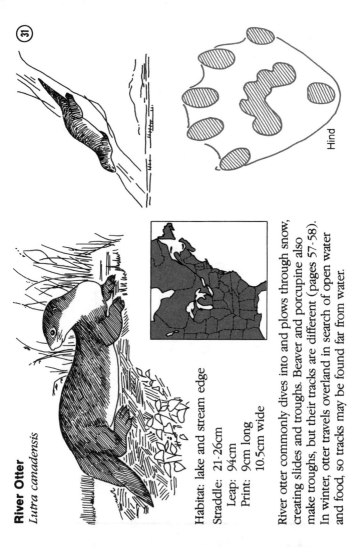

Hind

River Otter
Lutra canadensis

Habitat: lake and stream edge

Straddle: 21-26cm
Leap: 94cm
Print: 9cm long
10.5cm wide

River otter commonly dives into and plows through snow, creating slides and troughs. Beaver and porcupine also make troughs, but their tracks are different (pages 57-58). In winter, otter travels overland in search of open water and food, so tracks may be found far from water.

㉜ LEAPERS AND HOPPERS

Average straddle	Clues	Species
Less than 4cm	Tracks usually seen in winter	shrews, pocket mouse, p 34-35
4-5cm	Chipmunks hibernate; tracks uncommon in winter	white-footed mice, p 36-37 least chipmunk, p 33
5-8cm	Tracks uncommon in winter	eastern chipmunk, p 33 ground squirrels, p 40
6.5-9cm	Tracks grade into imperfect walker pattern; prints toed-in; tracks rarely seen in winter	spotted skunk, p 55
8-12cm	Tracks often lead to trees	red squirrel, p 39 flying squirrels, p 38
9-13cm	Tracks grade into imperfect walker pattern; prints very large compared to squirrel	raccoon, p 53
10-13cm	Individual toes usually do not show in print	rabbits, p 42-43
12-13cm	Tracks often lead to trees	gray squirrel, p 41 fox squirrel, p 41
18-21cm	Individual toes usually do not show in print	hares, p 44-45

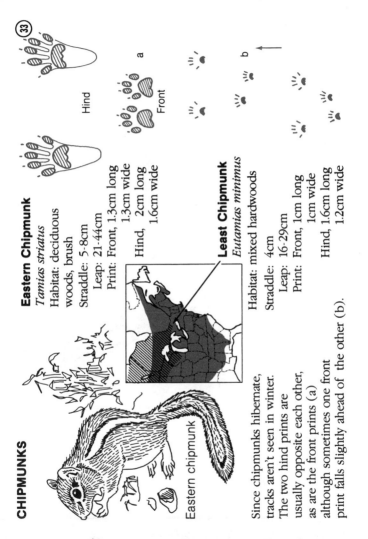

CHIPMUNKS

Eastern Chipmunk
Tamias striatus
Habitat: deciduous woods, brush
Straddle: 5-8cm
Leap: 21-44cm
Print: Front, 1.3cm long
1.3cm wide
Hind, 2cm long
1.6cm wide

Least Chipmunk
Eutamias minimus
Habitat: mixed hardwoods
Straddle: 4cm
Leap: 16-29cm
Print: Front, 1cm long
1cm wide
Hind, 1.6cm long
1.2cm wide

Eastern chipmunk

Since chipmunks hibernate, tracks aren't seen in winter. The two hind prints are usually opposite each other, as are the front prints (a) although sometimes one front print falls slightly ahead of the other (b).

Shorttail shrew

Shrew tracks are seen most often in snow. Their summer trails are lost in leaf litter. In loose snow, the feet drag between prints and the tail leaves a mark. Shrews habitually dive under snow. Prints and tracks of all shrews look the same; range and habitat give clues to identity of animal. Plains pocket mouse has the same pattern and straddle as shrews.

Pygmy Shrew
Microsorex hoyi
Habitat: open woods

Shorttail Shrew
Blarina brevicauda
Habitat: woods, brush, grass, marsh

For all shrews and plains pocket mouse:
Straddle: less than 4cm
Leap: variable
Print: 7mm long
7mm wide

In light snow

In loose snow

In deep snow

Masked Shrew
Sorex cinereus
Habitat: moist brush, field

Southeastern Shrew
Sorex longirostris
Habitat: moist woods, field

Plains Pocket Mouse
Perognathus flavescens
Habitat: prairie

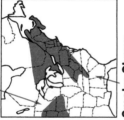

Smoky Shrew
Sorex fumeus
Habitat: birch, hemlock woods

Northern Water Shrew
Sorex palustris
Habitat: mountains in south,
stream edge in north

Longtail Shrew ⟶
Sorex dispar
Habitat: moist deciduous and
deciduous-coniferous woods

Arctic Shrew
Sorex arcticus
Habitat: bog, swamp

Least Shrew
Cryptotis parva
Habitat: field, marsh

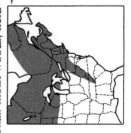

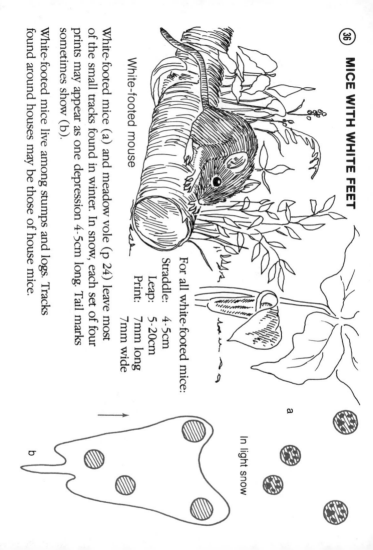

White-footed mouse

For all white-footed mice:
Straddle: 4-5cm
Leap: 5-20cm
Print: 7mm long
           7mm wide

White-footed mice (a) and meadow vole (p 24) leave most of the small tracks found in winter. In snow, each set of four prints may appear as one depression 4-5cm long. Tail marks sometimes show (b).

White-footed mice live among stumps and logs. Tracks found around houses may be those of house mice.

In light snow

a

b

White-footed Mouse
Peromyscus leucopus
Habitat: woods, brush

Deer Mouse
Peromyscus maniculatus
Habitat: woods, grass

Cotton Mouse
Peromyscus gossypinus
Habitat: woods, field and stream edge

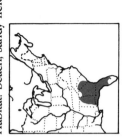

Brush Mouse
Peromyscus boylei
Habitat: rocky, dry areas

Golden Mouse
Peromyscus nuttali
Habitat: woods, canebrake

Oldfield Mouse
Peromyscus polionotus
Habitat: beach, sandy field

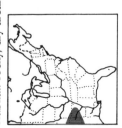

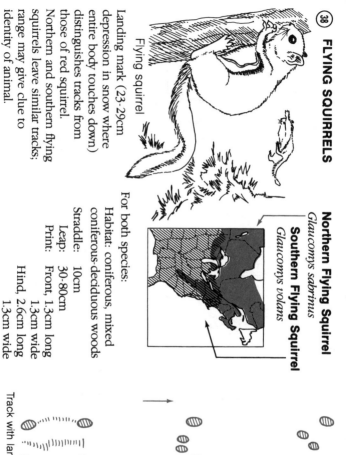

Flying squirrel

Northern Flying Squirrel
Glaucomys sabrinus

Southern Flying Squirrel
Glaucomys volans

For both species:

Habitat: coniferous, mixed coniferous-deciduous woods

Straddle: 10cm

Leap: 30-80cm

Print: Front, 1.3cm long
1.3cm wide
Hind, 2.6cm long
1.3cm wide

Track with landing mark

Landing mark (23-29cm depression in snow where entire body touches down) distinguishes tracks from those of red squirrel. Northern and southern flying squirrels leave similar tracks; range may give clue to identity of animal.

Red Squirrel
Tamiasciurus budsonicus

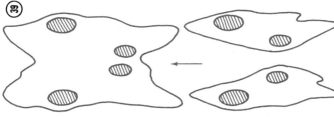

Habitat: coniferous, mixed
coniferous-deciduous
woods; swamp

Straddle: 8-12cm

Leap: 20-80cm

Print: Front, 1.3cm long
1.3cm wide
Hind, 2.6cm long
1.3cm wide

Tracks commonly lead from tree to tree. In snow, animal may make one depression (a) or two diamond-shaped marks (b). Red squirrel and gray squirrel usually place front feet next to each other rather than one in front of the other. (Compare with ground squirrel pattern, page 40.)

GROUND SQUIRRELS (GOPHERS)

Thirteen-lined Ground Squirrel (Gopher)

Citellus tridecimlineatus

Habitat: prairie, golf course

Straddle: 5cm

Leap: 7-10cm

Print: Front, 9-11mm long
5-7mm wide

Hind, 14-16cm long
1.1-1.3cm wide

Franklin Ground Squirrel, Gray Gopher

Citellus franklini

Habitat: open woods, tall grass, marsh edge

Straddle: 8cm

Leap: 12-17cm

Print: Front, 15-17cm long
1.2-1.4cm wide

Hind, 2.8-3cm long
2.2-2.4cm wide

Thirteen-lined ground squirrel

Ground squirrels generally occupy open country where there are no tree squirrels. Except in the south, ground squirrels hibernate, so tracks are not seen in mid-winter. The track pattern is elongated. Forefeet tend to land one in front of the other rather than next to each other. (Compare with pages 39 and 41.) Claws of ground squirrels are longer, straighter, and register more clearly than those of tree squirrels.

LARGE SQUIRRELS

Gray squirrel

Tracks are similar to red squirrel tracks (page 39) but prints and stride are larger. Heel registers fully in snow, but may not leave complete print in mud. Gray squirrel and fox squirrel tracks are similar; note range.

Eastern Fox Squirrel

Sciurus niger

Habitat: pines in south, open deciduous woods in north

Eastern Gray Squirrel

Sciurus carolinensis
Habitat: deciduous woods

For both species:
Straddle: 12-13cm
Leap: up to 94cm
Print: Front, 2.6cm long
            2.6cm wide
         Hind, 5.2cm long
            2.6cm wide

Track in light snow
(For deep snow pattern, see p 39.)

Track in mud

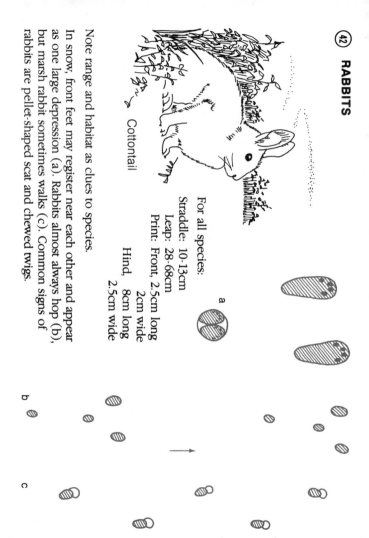

Cottontail

For all species:
Straddle: 10-13cm
Leap: 28-68cm
Print: Front, 2.5cm long
          2cm wide
Hind, 8cm long
          2.5cm wide

a

Note range and habitat as clues to species.
In snow, front feet may register near each other and appear as one large depression (a). Rabbits almost always hop (b), but marsh rabbit sometimes walks (c). Common signs of rabbits are pellet-shaped scat and chewed twigs.

b

c

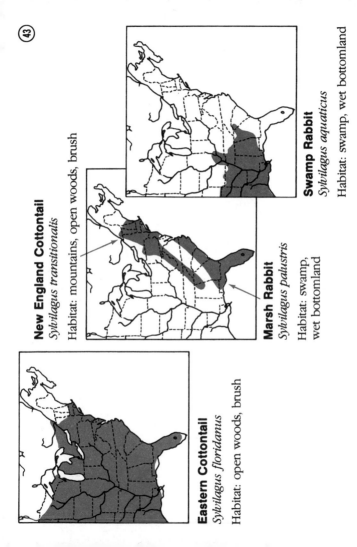

43

New England Cottontail
Sylvilagus transitionalis

Habitat: mountains, open woods, brush

Marsh Rabbit
Sylvilagus palustris

Habitat: swamp,
wet bottomland

Swamp Rabbit
Sylvilagus aquaticus

Habitat: swamp, wet bottomland

Eastern Cottontail
Sylvilagus floridanus

Habitat: open woods, brush

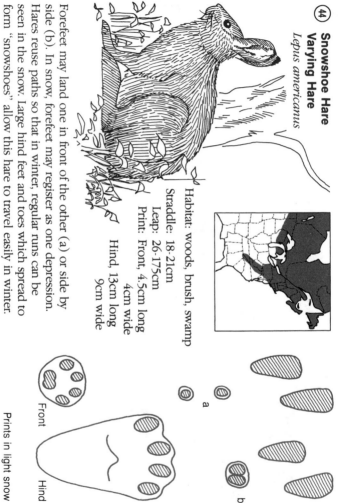

44 Snowshoe Hare
Varying Hare
Lepus americanus

Habitat: woods, brush, swamp
Straddle: 18-21cm
Leap: 26-175cm
Print: Front, 4.5cm long
4cm wide
Hind, 13cm long
9cm wide

Forefeet may land one in front of the other (a) or side by side (b). In snow, forefeet may register as one depression. Hares reuse paths so that in winter, regular runs can be seen in the snow. Large hind feet and toes which spread to form "snowshoes" allow this hare to travel easily in winter.

Front

Hind

Prints in light snow

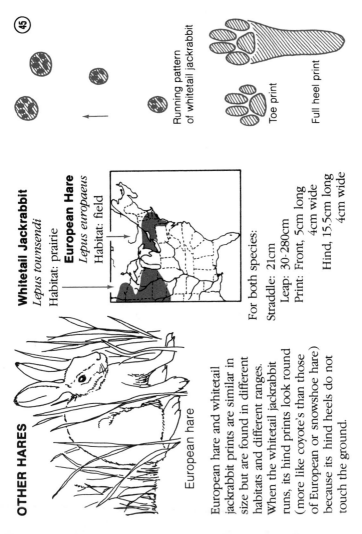

Running pattern
of whitetail jackrabbit

Toe print

Full heel print

OTHER HARES

Whitetail Jackrabbit
Lepus townsendi
Habitat: prairie

European Hare
Lepus europaeus
Habitat: field

For both species:
Straddle: 21cm
Leap: 30-280cm
Print: Front, 5cm long
4cm wide
Hind, 15.5cm long
4cm wide

European hare

European hare and whitetail
jackrabbit prints are similar in
size but are found in different
habitats and different ranges.
When the whitetail jackrabbit
runs, its hind prints look round
(more like coyote's than those
of European or snowshoe hare)
because its hind heels do not
touch the ground.

Average straddle	Clues	Species
3.5-4cm	Tracks found in marsh	rice rat, cotton rat, wood rat, p 48-49
6.5-9cm	Tracks meandering through field and woods; prints toed-in	striped skunk, p 52 spotted skunk, p 53
9cm	Tracks found near and leading into water; tail drag evident	muskrat, p 50
10.5cm	Tracks may lead to tree; tail drag may show	opossum, p 51
9-13cm	Woodchuck hibernates in winter; raccoon doesn't	woodchuck, p 54 raccoon, p 55
10.5-18cm	Extremely toed-in print; tracks found in prairie or midwest golf course	badger, p 56
15.5-21cm	Tracks found near and leading into water; dam or lodge nearby	beaver, p 58
21-23.5cm	Toed-in prints; hemlock twigs littering ground	porcupine, p 57
36cm	Very large prints!	black bear, p 59

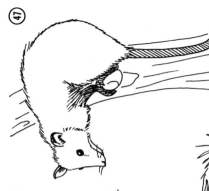

As a group, imperfect walkers are heavyset and move with a slow, lumbering gait. They gallop briefly, if at all. Because they lack speed and agility, they must escape predators by other means.

Beavers and muskrats can swim away.

Raccoons, opossums, and porcupines can climb trees.

Badgers and woodchucks can burrow into the ground.

Some have other defensive adaptations.

Porcupines have quills.

Badgers, members of the weasel family, have very sharp claws and teeth.

Skunks, also in the weasel family, have an offensive spray.

Bounders are mostly weasels and hoppers are mostly rodents, but imperfect walkers are a mixed group of animals from many families (see page 60).

Eastern wood rat

Tracks of cotton, rice, and eastern wood rats are similar. Habitat, range, and print size provide helpful clues. Norway rat is found in the city. Black rat is sometimes found in fields, but usually near buildings.

Hind and front prints (a), overlapped prints of walking gait (b), and running gait (c).

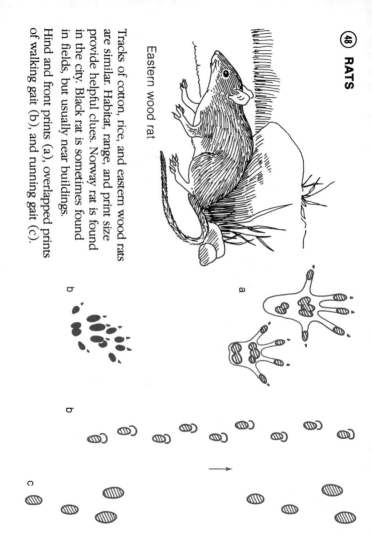

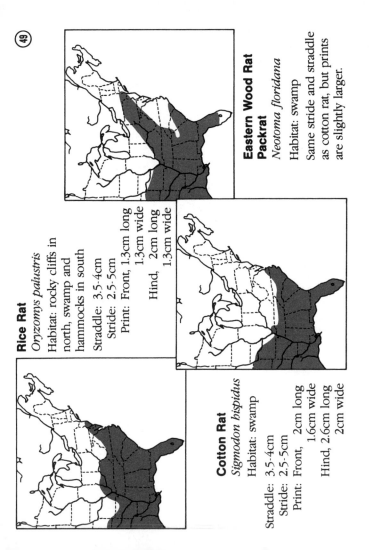

Rice Rat
Oryzomys palustris
Habitat: rocky cliffs in north, swamp and hammocks in south

Straddle: 3.5-4cm
Stride: 2.5-5cm
Print: Front, 1.3cm long
1.3cm wide
Hind, 2cm long
1.3cm wide

Cotton Rat
Sigmodon hispidus
Habitat: swamp

Straddle: 3.5-4cm
Stride: 2.5-5cm
Print: Front, 2cm long
1.6cm wide
Hind, 2.6cm long
2cm wide

Eastern Wood Rat
Packrat
Neotoma floridana
Habitat: swamp
Same stride and straddle as cotton rat, but prints are slightly larger.

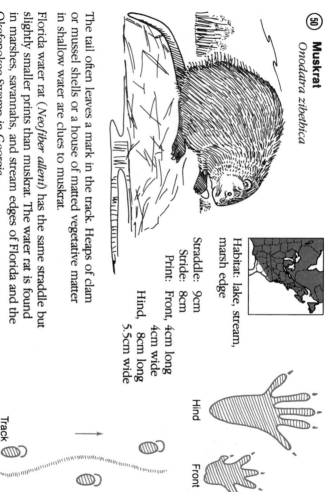

50 Muskrat
Onodatra zibethica

Habitat: lake, stream, marsh edge

Straddle: 9cm
Stride: 8cm
Print: Front, 4cm long
4cm wide
Hind, 8cm long
5.5cm wide

Hind

Front

Track

The tail often leaves a mark in the track. Heaps of clam or mussel shells or a house of matted vegetative matter in shallow water are clues to muskrat.

Florida water rat (*Neofiber alleni*) has the same straddle but slightly smaller prints than muskrat. The water rat is found in marshes, savannahs, and stream edges of Florida and the Okefenokee Swamp in Georgia.

Front

Hind

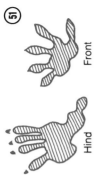

Walking

Opossum
Didelphis marsupialis

Habitat: open woods

Straddle: 10.5cm
Stride: 18cm
Print: Front, 5cm long
5cm wide
Hind, 6cm long
4cm wide

Opossum is a tree climber, so tracks may lead to trees.
Opossum track is similar to raccoon track, but opossum
hind prints show one toe which slants inward. Tail
sometimes leaves mark.

Striped Skunk
Mephitis mephitis

Habitat: woods, field, suburbs
Straddle: 6.5-9cm
Stride: variable
Print: Front, 2cm   long
       2.5cm wide
       Hind, 4cm   long
       2.5cm wide

Toes point in slightly. Forefoot is placed just ahead of hind foot. Claws on forefeet are large and used for digging. Claw marks often show in fore prints, but seldom in hind prints. Striped skunk is inactive in winter but may wander during a warm spell.

Hind

Front

Loping

Walking

Galloping

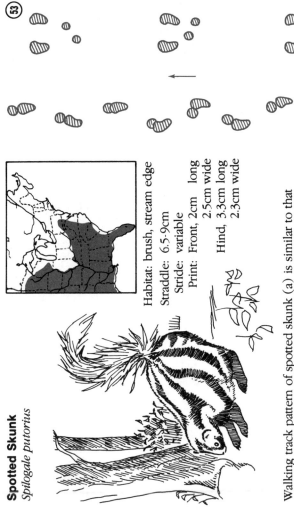

Spotted Skunk
Spilogale putorius

Habitat: brush, stream edge
Straddle: 6.5-9cm
Stride: variable
Print: Front, 2cm long
            2.5cm wide
        Hind, 3.3cm long
            2.3cm wide

Walking track pattern of spotted skunk (a) is similar to that of striped skunk. When moving quickly, spotted skunk hops (b) rather than gallops. Tracks are like squirrel's but the prints are more stub-toed.

Woodchuck
Marmota monax

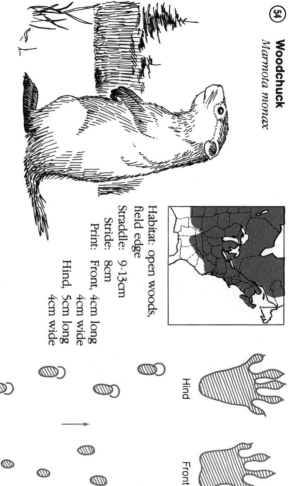

Habitat: open woods, field edge

Straddle: 9-13cm
Stride: 8cm
Print: Front, 4cm long
4cm wide
Hind, 5cm long
4cm wide

Hind foot registers near front print; often hind heel does not register. Woodchucks hibernate. Woodchuck has four toes on front foot; raccoon has five.

Hind

Front

Walking

Running

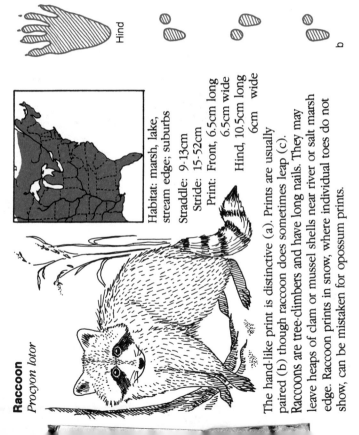

Raccoon
Procyon lotor

Habitat: marsh, lake, stream edge; suburbs

Straddle: 9-13cm

Stride: 15-52cm

Print: Front, 6.5cm long
6.5cm wide
Hind, 10.5cm long
6cm wide

a — Hind / Front

b

c

The hand-like print is distinctive (a). Prints are usually paired (b) though raccoon does sometimes leap (c). Raccoons are tree-climbers and have long nails. They may leave heaps of clam or mussel shells near river or salt marsh edge. Raccoon prints in snow, where individual toes do not show, can be mistaken for opossum prints.

Badger
Taxidea taxus

Habitat: prairie, golf course

Straddle: 10.5-18cm

Stride: 15.5-31cm

Print: Front, 6.5cm long
        9cm   wide
      Hind, 5cm   long
        5cm   wide

Prints are extremely toed-in (a). Long digging claws on front feet usually show in prints. Badger tracks resemble skunk tracks but badger has a much wider straddle and larger prints.

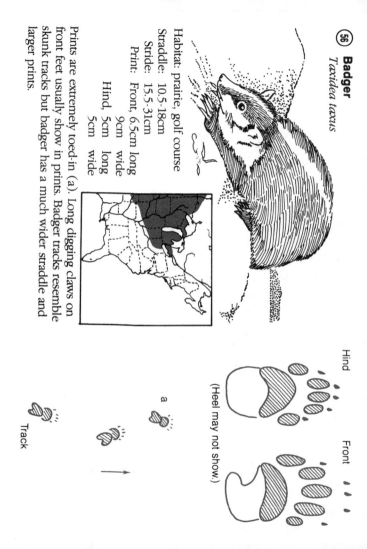

Hind

Front

(Heel may not show.)

a

Track

Porcupine
Erethizon dorsatum

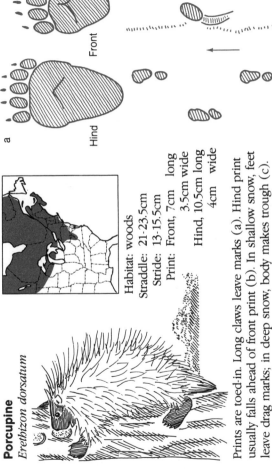

Front

Hind

a

b

c

Habitat: woods
Straddle: 21-23.5cm
Stride: 13-15.5cm
Print: Front, 7cm long
3.5cm wide
Hind, 10.5cm long
4cm wide

Prints are toed-in. Long claws leave marks (a). Hind print usually falls ahead of front print (b). In shallow snow, feet leave drag marks; in deep snow, body makes trough (c). In dust or snow, tail may leave whisk-broom type sweeps.

During winter, porcupine often stays in or near one tree. Hemlock is a favorite. The ground below is littered with nipped-off twigs and scat.

Beaver
Castor canadensis

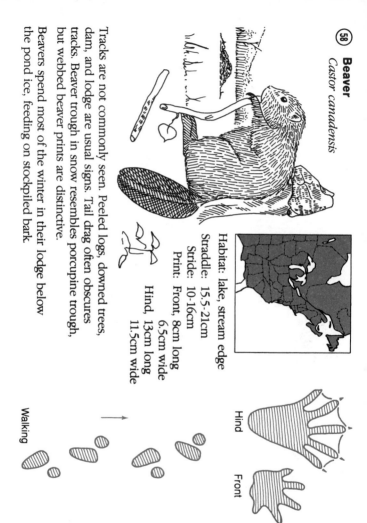

Habitat: lake, stream edge
Straddle: 15.5-21cm
Stride: 10-16cm
Print: Front, 8cm long
            6.5cm wide
        Hind, 13cm long
            11.5cm wide

Tracks are not commonly seen. Peeled logs, downed trees, dam, and lodge are usual signs. Tail drag often obscures tracks. Beaver trough in snow resembles porcupine trough, but webbed beaver prints are distinctive.

Beavers spend most of the winter in their lodge below the pond ice, feeding on stockpiled bark.

Hind

Front

Walking

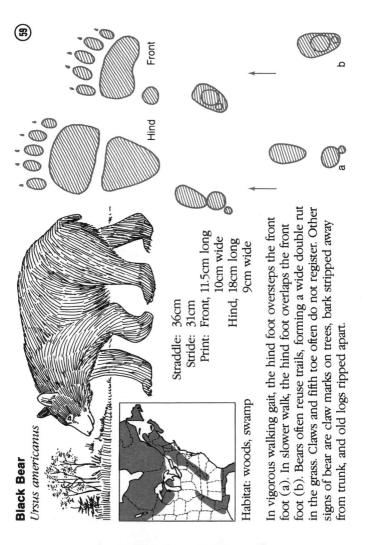

Front

Hind

Black Bear
Ursus americanus

Straddle: 36cm
Stride: 31cm
Print: Front, 11.5cm long
10cm wide
Hind, 18cm long
9cm wide

Habitat: woods, swamp

In vigorous walking gait, the hind foot oversteps the front foot (a). In slower walk, the hind foot overlaps the front foot (b). Bears often reuse trails, forming a wide double rut in the grass. Claws and fifth toe often do not register. Other signs of bear are claw marks on trees, bark stripped away from trunk, and old logs ripped apart.

Pouched mammals: Order *Marsupialia*
  Family *Didelphidae:*   opossum

Insect-eaters: Order *Insectivora*
  Family *Soricidae:*   shrews

Flesh-eaters: Order *Carnivora*
  Family *Ursidae:*   black bear
  Family *Procyonidae:*   raccoon
  Family *Mustelidae:*   weasels
    mink
    marten
    fisher
    otter
    badger
    skunks
  Family *Canidae:*   foxes
    coyote
    wolf
  Family *Felidae:*   bobcat
    lynx
    mountain lion

Gnawing mammals:
  Family *Sciuridae:*   Order *Rodentia*
    chipmunk
    ground squirrels
    tree squirrels
    woodchuck

  Family *Heteromyidae:*   pocket mouse
  Family *Castoridae:*   beaver
  Family *Cricetidae:*   mice
    rats
    lemmings
    voles
    muskrat
    water rat

  Family *Erethizontidae:* porcupine

Rabbits and hares: Order *Lagomorpha*
  Family *Leporidae:*   rabbits
    hares

Hoofed mammals: Order *Artiodactyla*
  Family *Cervidae:*   deer
    moose

Index

Other books in the pocket-sized "finder" series:

for U.S. and Canada
east of the Rockies

TREE FINDER - native and common introduced trees
FLOWER FINDER - spring wildflowers & flower families
WINTER TREE FINDER - leafless winter trees
FERN FINDER - native ferns of the Midwest and Northeast
BERRY FINDER - native plants with fleshy fruits
TRACK FINDER - tracks and footprints of mammals
LIFE ON INTERTIDAL ROCKS - organisms of North Atlantic coast
WINTER WEED FINDER - dry plant structures in winter

for the Pacific Coast

PACIFIC COAST TREE FINDER - native trees, Sitka to San Diego
REDWOOD REGION FLOWER FINDER - wildflowers of the coastal fog belt
PACIFIC COAST MAMMALS - mammals, their tracks, other signs

for Rocky Mtn. and
desert states

ROCKY MOUNTAIN TREE FINDER - native Rocky Mountain trees
ROCKY MOUNTAIN FLOWER FINDER - wildflowers below tree line
MOUNTAIN STATE MAMMALS - mammals, their tracks, skulls, and scat

for Stargazers

CONSTELLATION FINDER - patterns in the night sky and star stories

NATURE STUDY GUIDES are published by KEEN COMMUNICATIONS, PO Box 43673, Birmingham, AL 35243 (888) 604-4537, naturestudy.com. SEE keencommunication.com for our full line of outdoor activity guides by MENASHA RIDGE PRESS and WILDERNESS PRESS. Including regional and national parks hiking, camping, backpacking, and more.